COACHIN PERFORMANCE IMPROVEMENT

T0290582

Jack Ramsay
Jim Lynch

Foreword by Sean Covey

University Press of America,® Inc.
Dallas · Lanham · Boulder · New York · Oxford

Copyright © 2004 by
University Press of America,® Inc.
4501 Forbes Boulevard
Suite 200
Lanham, Maryland 20706
UPA Acquisitions Department (301) 459-3366

PO Box 317
Oxford
OX2 9RU, UK

Library of Congress Control Number: 2004105685
ISBN 0-7618-2805-2 (paperback : alk. ppr.)

We dedicate this book to those leaders who have come before us, those who have inspired us, those who continue to challenge us and the people who we come in contact with that allow us to use our acquired skills.

CONTENTS

FOREWORD   *vii*

PREFACE   *ix*

          Making the connection

CHAPTER 1   **SO YOU WANT TO BE A LEADER**   1
                 • What to do to be Successful
                 • Achievement
                 • Knowledge
                 • Talent
                 • Leadership Qualities
                 • Success vs. Failure

CHAPTER 2   **HOW TO MAKE A WINNING TEAM**   5
                 • Motivating for Improvement
                 • Vision
                 • Game Plan
                 • Personnel
                 • Selection
                 • Development
                 • Establishment of Goals
                 • Playing the Game
                 • Evaluation
                 • The Future

CHAPTER 3   **GOAL SETTING**   13
                 • Setting up the Plan
                 • Goal Setting
                 • Types of Goals
                 • Examples of Goal Setting

CHAPTER 4   **FEEDBACK**   17
- Effective Timeouts
- Making Adjustments
- Conducting Meetings
- Feedback
- Offering Criticism
- Personalization
- Style

CHAPTER 5   **THE TEAM**   23
- The Final Result
- Teamwork
- Establishing Teamwork
- Healthy vs. Unhealthy
- Evaluation of Teamwork

CHAPTER 6   **WHAT'S NEXT?**   29
- What to do in the off season
- Control Theory
- Satisfaction of needs
- Self Evaluation
- Servant Leadership
- Stress Management
- Self-fulfilling Prophecy

APPENDIX   **THE CORE OF LEADERSHIP**   33

AFTERWORD   37

TAO OF LEADERSHIP   43

BIBLIOGRAPHY   45

ABOUT THE AUTHORS   47

FOREWORD

I met Jim Lynch in 1996 when a colleague suggested that I talk to "The Lone Wolf" as Jim was lovingly referred to. I was excited to meet and talk with Jim because I had heard many stories of his commitment to improving the lives of others through leadership training and personal modeling of the principles. And one of the things I found appealing about Jim was that he had proactively already begun to adapt the 7Habits to youth at about the same time I was beginning to write my book, *The 7 Habits of Highly Effective Teens*.

Since that first meeting, Jim and I have developed and maintained a strong win-win relationship including co-presenting at events and picking Jim's brain about teens and teen life changes. Over the years I have found Jim to be the real deal as he seeks to find ways to challenge himself and others to be the best they can be.

In my college days I played some football and I love the sport but any athlete worth his salt follows and appreciates all great athletes and coaches of other sports. And anyone who has ever been involved in the great sport of basketball, at any level, knows the name Dr. Jack Ramsay. Although I do not personally know Jack, what I do know from my reading and experiences related to me from others, is that he too is a man who models what he teaches. That makes him the real deal to me. Jack's career spans many years at many levels and at all levels there is only respect and admiration, not only for his knowledge of the game of basketball, but more specifically, his ability to lead people.

In addition to the careers these men are now following, they are teachers in the purest form- they practice what they teach. And what they teach you will find in this little, yet powerful, book. What this book teaches us is that there is never just one way of doing things. Now, Jack and Jim are forthright in telling us that this concept and these ideas are not new, but I'd like to challenge them on that. What is new and different about this book is that they try to put academic theories, studies and models into simple applications through the analogy of basketball! And then they make that basketball analogy applicable to where you are and what you do- even if you don't like basketball!

Jack and Jim have put together a solid expression of how to lead regardless of the role you are playing. They have used the theories of others and blended that with life lessons and experiences to make it meaningful to all of us.

What they have brought to us has great relevance in this chaotic and frenetic world in which we live and work. The values they espouse and live in their own lives and the insights they are willing to share can help us all create meaningful and enduring win-win relationships with anyone.

I am pleased that they have, by example, incorporated into their lives what they have learned, brought it together in a clear, concise and fun manner, and are willing to share it. Trust me, the book, like the authors, is the real deal.

I invite you to enjoy their story, and to take it to heart and apply it to becoming a better leader and person.

Sean Covey, Author
The 7Habits of Highly Effective Teens

PREFACE

Making the Connection

Tracing American interest in sports to its origins is to go back to ancient Greece. The lure that the Olympic Games hold today was just as big at its beginning in 776 B.C. The ancient philosopher, Plato, himself a wrestler, saw sports as a way to harden the spirit so that the "artists" would not be so softened that they would be rendered ineffective. Throughout history this fascination with sports had its ups and downs, but with the onset of the Jeffersonian Era sports were in American culture to stay. Sports, as seen through the British traditions that America was built upon, builds great moral character. American general, Douglas MacArthur clearly stated this connection when he said, "Upon the fields of friendly strife are sown the seed that, upon other fields, on other days, will bear the fruits of victory." Chief Executive Officers may have long forgotten what they've learned in high school calculus class or college biology class, but can speak in no uncertain terms of their sports endeavors and even cite scores of specific games from many years ago. The business world through its sponsorships, the American public, through its interest and managers, at all levels continue these traditions into the 2000's. Americans are fascinated by sports. Businessmen read the sports pages after reading the business section in the newspaper. Many even read about the sports news before turning to their business information. Sports terms are used in business meetings every day. Strike-out is synonymous with failure, time-out means let's reflect on what we're doing, let's be more like a team making it seem that a team breeds success, or it's time to throw them a curve implying in the business world - - let's confuse them.

This is not a book that serves as an expose of the National Basketball Association or a book of how to's but rather a practical book on leading. It uses examples of how a professional coach, coaching the best players at their sport in the world, still serves as a manager of people. In sports, as in business, the leading of people is crucial for success. Success in sports depends on having the right people to do the job, having a winning season, minimizing your losses, efficient use of time and measuring success through the bottom line - - the standings at the end of the season. This sounds a lot like business ventures where you need the best materials and the best personnel to make and deliver your product in the most timely fashion with the least amount of waste without sacrificing quality for a profit. The only way in sports or business you can have success is to have dedicated and knowledgeable coaches or leaders who can get to the bottom line effectively and efficiently through the use of the team or company's primary resource needed for success - - people. What follows are examples of what works in the coaching of highly skilled athletes and relates these techniques to coaching people in the business world to improve success.

Jack Ramsay
Jim Lynch

CHAPTER 1

SO YOU WANT TO BE A LEADER

Better than Fame, is still the wish for Fame,
the constant training for a glorious strife.
Edward, Lord Lytton
"The Athlete"

A manager is like a groom at a wedding - - you have to have one, but nobody really pays too much attention to him, unless of course, he's a coach and losing a lot of games. In that case, we're reminded about what Henry the Eighth was alleged to have said to his fourth wife, "Don't worry, I won't keep you long."

In sports or business, you are often witness to great levels of achievement. A wide range of talent is used to attain this achievement and everyone hopes that he's a part of the talent pool. Some people have a lot of talent and use it, some people have a lot of talent and waste it and some people have a marginal level of talent but bleed every drop of potential from it and achieve great things. A leader must be aware that personal and professional growth is a blend of talent and determination and takes place over a period of time. There needs to be an awareness of where you were, where you are right now and where you want to go. There is also the need for the desire and belief that once you reach a particular point, you can go beyond it to reach bigger and better achievements. Alexander Pope, the 18th century English poet-philosopher wrote, "A little learning is a dangerous thing, so drink deep of the Pyrean spring, there, shallow drafts intoxicate the brain while drinking largely sobers us again." In Greek mythology, the Pyrean Mountains were an area in Macedonia where the muses went to drink to get inspiration for their overseeing of the arts. Alexander Pope saw in this an axiom that all of us can take heed as a future leader - - the need to gain knowledge. In this regard, we have to remember that a smattering of knowledge can only get us into trouble because sips tend to only intoxicate us and make us act foolishly. If we seek to gain all the knowledge we can, if we drink deeply of the Pyrean spring, we have true knowledge and it gives us a base on which to operate.

There are many ways to gain knowledge, from a textbook, through travel, from experience and through human interaction. Since knowledge is at the base of where we are and where we're going, we need to delve into our make-up to get a good look at our talents. If we look at the make-up of some very talented people, we may glean some insight that can help us set the stages for our personal success.

Former New York Knicks star and former United States Senator from New Jersey, Bill Bradley, can serve to show us that, with intense dedication and practice, you can become whatever you want to be. Bradley entered the NBA after an outstanding academic and athletic career at Princeton University and two years off from basketball as a Rhoads Scholar at Oxford University. He didn't have great natural basketball ability, but through hours of practice and a burning desire to be the best, he became an integral part of the world championship teams of the Knicks. Itzhak Perlman, a world renowned violinist, overcame severe physical disability to be one of the best violinists ever. David Halberstam, a Pulitzer Prize winning author, is a timeless researcher. He seeks out all the facts, uncovers every pertinent detail about his subjects, and only then does he collate these data into his interesting literary style. Iron Man Champion, Paula Newby-Frazer, didn't become the best woman tri-athlete in the world by accident. Her achievement came from precise skill development and endless hours of just plain hard work.

Magic Johnson, maestro of the Los Angeles Lakers' great success in the '80's, is a classic case of determination to succeed. At the beginning of his NBA career there were limitations to his game. Magic, a dominant right handed player was stymied when forced to go to his left. It threw off his whole game. He lacked the creativity he showed when driving, passing and shooting with his right hand. During his first season, when playing against the Portland TrailBlazers, Magic was sometimes responsible for as many as nine turnovers in a game because he was forcing unsuccessful passes from the left side of the floor. But after a summer of working on his left handed skills, Magic overcame this shortcoming and it never seriously hampered him again. Magic Johnson isn't hung up on gaining personal statistics, unless they benefit his team. Each new season, he improved some facet of his game that makes his team better.

There are many other very talented individuals from all walks of life, people like former President Richard Nixon, former presidential candidate and United States Senator Gary Hart, rock star vocalist Janice Joplan, NBA All Star player Michael Ray Richardson and others. What happened to them? Nixon, facing impeachment proceedings, resigned from office in 1974. Hart dropped out of the presidential race in 1984 because of personal improprieties. Joplan died of a drug overdose. Richardson had more basketball talent than Bill Bradley and almost as much as Magic Johnson, but he had to go to Italy to play basketball because he couldn't withstand the pressures of the NBA and turned to substance abuse. Each of these individuals had great talent and wonderful opportunities, but allowed outside influences to alter the direction of their lives.

As leaders, we can learn from these examples by trying to explain the differences between these two sets of people. Dr. Bruce Ogilvie, a father of sports psychology, may be able to shed some light on how we can plan for our success. Bruce was used by the TrailBlazers to help the coaching staff understand the players and help the players understand themselves and thereby, enhance their performance. Once Ogilvie was asked to define what were the characteristics of successful leaders. He responded with three points that can serve us as potential leaders. First, top executives possess an insatiable drive to succeed. In sports this drive would be to win, in academics to be the most knowledgeable, in business to have the greatest profit and in an industrial setting, to have the greatest output of a product at a Six Sigma or higher level. Second, there is a great curiosity about his job. There is a deep desire to learn, to acquire the knowledge needed for the job, or to paraphrase Pope, to drink deep or taste not the Pyrean spring. Third, there is the ability to be psychologically transparent. This is the quality that permits us to be straightforward in dealing with others, and to always act in the same manner in all types of situations.

If you want to be a leader, you have to plan for it; you have to think about it. Leadership takes courage. Knowledge provides a solid base for the courage, while the three components for success help you to make the most of the opportunities that come along. Someone once said, "The harder I work, the luckier I get." There is a lot of truth in this simple maxim - - so let's get started!

CHAPTER 2

HOW TO MAKE A WINNING TEAM

The Sword is great, but he rules by hate, rules
with a bloody hand:
Honesty, peace, and comradeship are features
of my command!
Edward Verral Lucas
"The Cricket Bat Sings"

In Japan, the Bushido Code of Honor governs the life of the Samurai. In modern Japan, the Samurai's run their business under this code of teamwork - - do your best, but be sure to do your best for the group. This Samurai code is based on obedience, dedication, making the supreme effort, loyalty and spirit. With modification to fit our culture, these standards can be a team's code of ethics and help increase overall effectiveness. As leaders, we can instill these values into our team. Before a leader can gain this type of commitment from his employees, some very important details need to be attended to.The first step toward successful managing is to firmly establish a vision by which to operate. A vision is an expression of the general principles which govern an organization. As such, it contains a statement of objectives as well as a general plan for reaching those objectives. A vision, therefore, states in general terms what the leader expects from himself and his team members.

A basketball coach might have a vision that states that his team will play a fast-paced game, emphasizing an aggressive pressing defense and a fast breaking offense in order to win. Practice sessions are organized so that every activity that the players experience stresses the characteristics of the pressing defense and the fast break offense. By repeated physical experiences, the players become part of the vision. It becomes how they play the game of basketball. They become exponents of the vision of the coach.

The team carries this vision into the game. It becomes their "style" of play. Their opponents scout them to see how they play and attempt to nullify their objectives. The media may even label the team with an application related to their style. The Boston Celtics were known as "The Green Wave" when they were fast breaking their way to eight straight NBA championships. Coach Dick Harter had a University of Oregon team known as the "Kamikaze Kids" because of their do or die defense. The NBA Lakers of the 1980's were called "Show Time" because of their flamboyant style. Each was a style of play that served to implement the team's vision.

Ideally, if the vision is sound, well-planned and carried out effectively by the players, the result is victories or success in competition. The players are able to relate this success to the vision. They develop a certain pride in being members of the team and it its style of play. They are the team and the team is them. The team and the players are one.

Success is euphoric. Everyone enjoys it and strives to attain it. A sound vision carefully expounded and realistically applied, leads individuals to the realization of their goals. The objective of the leader, then, is to be the leader who sets and models the style which the team uses to fulfill its vision. The style selected to implement a vision cannot be developed haphazardly. It must be effective and productive. A style is developed through personal experience, observation of other successful styles, and through theoretical applications. Through a synthesis of these facts, a personal style is derived that leads to the attainment of the vision. The more personal their style, the more investment of self that it contains, the greater its chances for success.

The next step toward becoming a successful leader is to select the kind of personnel that will help implement the vision and "fit" the style selected. In basketball, if the vision calls for a pressing defense and a fast break offense, the team obviously needs quick-footed personnel with aggressive personalities (A seven foot shot blocker wouldn't hurt either!).

Every draft selection, each trade that is consummated and all free agents signings are made with those characteristics in mind. There is also an awareness of the roles that each of these players will fill on the team. Physical skills are judged through close observation of the players on a number of occasions. Personality judgments are more difficult to make. A method used by the Portland TrailBlazers to determine personal characteristics was to administer the Athletic Motivational Inventory (AMI) to each player. The results of this inventory were also used to help select personnel. For example, if there were five players whom the Blazers thought they would have the opportunity to draft, the five were brought to Portland before the draft, given a physical exam, a test of physical performance, to determine foot speed, reaction time and jumping ability, the AMI and were interviewed by the head coach. This information, along with observations of the player in games formed the basis on which players were drafted.

The AMI revealed pertinent general tendencies of the individual in the areas of aggression, drive, responsibility, trust, coach ability, determination, emotional control, tough-mindedness, self confidence and leadership. Rarely did the inventory turn out findings that did not hold up in actual experience. This test was administered by Dr. Ogilvie. Ogilvie would then sit with each player and the Blazer coach and review the test findings. It was a great help to the coach and the players to know in which areas there was strength and which areas needed improvement. Players with strong readings across the board were certain to be valuable team players.

Players in general liked the test and enjoyed the critiques with Ogilvie and the coach. At one such session with Kermit Washington, Bruce related to Kermit what the test revealed about his psychological make-up. As the psychologist progressed, Kermit began to smile and nod in agreement. As Ogilvie concluded, Washington said, "That's me. You really got me."

The inventory was an excellent tool for helping the player to better understand himself and, to learn how he could improve psychologically. It also afforded the coach the opportunity to: 1) Understand the player more quickly than usual; 2) Utilize the player's strengths and; 3) Treat his weaknesses more carefully. The coach also had the opportunity at these meetings to give the player suggestions for using his qualities in basketball situations. For example, a player with strong aggression tendencies was encouraged to become the catalyst for the team's physical style of play, diving for loose balls, taking defensive charges, blocking out aggressively or pressing hard against an opponent dribbling in the backcourt. He becomes a team leader in this respect and subtly induces others to become more aggressive with their plays.

Just as the AMI is available to test athletes, many assessments are available for business use. The Management Effectiveness Profile System (MEPS) is an example of an inventory which measures leadership style. The NEO Five-Factor Inventory (NEO-FFI) measures the fit between personality and behavior and types of jobs. These and many other types of instruments, designed for specific purposes, assist leaders in making decision regarding the hiring of new personnel and the assigning of roles to specific employees. Industrial psychology should be used by leaders as a component in their decision-making process just as the sports psychologist can assist the coach in the sports arena.

The next area of concern for the leader is determining the roles to be played by the personnel selected. A good team is one in which all members are utilizing their individual skills and talents to reach a common goals. In basketball there are the guards who form the first line of defense, handle the ball and play-making chores, and score mostly from the perimeter. The big men defend the basket area, rebound the ball, and block shots. On offense, they run to fill fast break lanes and score mostly in the area from the free throw line extended to the baseline. It is vital to team success for these general roles to be stressed by the coach and observed and honored by the players. The team cannot succeed if the guards can't stop the opponent from penetrating with the ball or if the big men persist in dribbling the ball and shooting from the perimeter.

The coach must select his best players to fill the various starting roles and then drill them hard to be certain that they are able to carry out their tasks. Reserve players known as back ups or role players are identified and given a general plan for how and when they will be used in the game situation. It is sound practice for the new coach of a team to meet with each player to relate his philosophy and how he plans to utilize the player's talents. At such a meeting of player and coach at Portland, Bill Walton listened intently, gave some input of his own and then as the meeting concluded he said, "There's one more thing coach. Don't assume that we know anything." Walton was stressing the team's need of fundamental emphasis. The TrailBlazers had not made the playoffs at that point in the six year history. That season, 1977, the Blazers were NBA champions. That team was comprised players who had excellent team attitudes and who accepted their roles extremely well. It was a "hungry" team - - one which had not known success, but thought it could achieve more than it had done before. It was a team whose confidence grew as the season continued, so that in the final series against the Philadelphia 76ers, it had the inner strength and resolve to overcome losing the first two games. The final result was a 4 – 2 Portland series victory.

During the late 1980's, the Detroit Pistons can be viewed as a model in which to emulate. The Pistons during this period have fully utilized their personnel by matching each player to the best possible role that they can play to foster team success. The starting players, Isaiah Thomas, Joe Dumars, Dennis Rodman, John Salley and Bill Lambeer, all accept the positions they are to play and play the position with reckless abandon. Combine these starters with a bench full of backups, who play their role when called upon, the Pistons have sustained themselves as champions in the NBA. Each of these team players, although not all all-stars or hall of famers, are used in such a manner by the coach to their maximum potential. In the true Samurai manner, each individual plays for the team not for themselves. The past success of the TrailBlazers and indeed all championship teams is due to everyone having a role and carrying it out. Championship teams have a coach who motivates each player to maximize his potential to benefit the team. Sometimes when coaches or managers inherit groups, the personnel is already in place. In these cases, the coach needs to make adjustments in the game plan in order to gain all out effort from the players while insisting on teamwork. If a full court press was in the original game plane, and the talent was inadequate, an adjustment to a half-court press might maximize the players available. Meanwhile, the coach seeks other players to carry out the game plan he wants. In this case, it may be necessary to delete reluctant participants and purge those who won't come on board or buy into the game plan. Baseball immortal, Casey Stengel, once said, "The key to success as a manager is to keep separate those that hate you from those who haven't made up their mind yet." A leader does not have to be liked but needs to be respected. If the people you are leading like you consider it a bonus.

In a positive situation, the team sees the actions of the coach helping them become more successful. The coach becomes accepted as the leader. He may be seen as a shrill or taskmaster or a quiet, low-key director. So long as he is consistent, he will be accepted for who he is and often the player will model the coach's behavior. This helps to establish a rapport with the team. In this regard, it is important not to give mixed messages - - like expecting the players to keep their composure while the coach loses his. The players also look to the coach to develop their skills so that they are better able to fit into the game plan. The coach works on the premise that everyone wants to be better. If they coach can show the players how they can be better, respect for the coach, develops. The player's confidence builds and there is the potential for great rapport between player and coach. The coach guides the players to excellence through skill development and fosters the player's belief in themselves.

Over time, the coach further defines and refines the players' roles. Performance on a daily basis - - in athletics, at practice or in game - - may dictate a certain role of a player. In business, your plan is tested every day and in the NBA it may be tested as many as four times a week. In each case, the opponent always has the same objective as you have - - to be the best. This means that situations might arise and although you may have set expectations for players, these expectations may change. In the basketball planning stages, it is critical that the starters recognize their roles: the playmakers, the small forwards and the big man. But, just as important, are the reserves like John Havlichek, Frank Ramsey, Michael Cooper, and Vinnie Johnson. Each needs to understand his role and accepts that this is the most beneficial role they can play for the team. The coach needs to set the tone that roles are generally set, but may be adjusted if a player is not doing what's best for the team. Willingness to modify the game plan without going against the overall plan fosters a players' trust in the coach. For example, when playing the Los Angeles Lakers the initial game plan may call to double team

Shaquille O'Neill. The coach notices that on this given night, O'Neill is passing very well for easy scores so that he modifies the game plan to play with single coverage and later in the game might go back to the double team.

After the test or the game, player performance needs to be evaluated. In sports this has become facilitated by the use of videotape. The game may be re-run and dissected over and over again. In business, we need to be just as explicit and we'll have to resort to constant note taking on our team members and data analysis on performance. It's vital to keep records or we might miss seeing a player dribbling the ball too much. A point guard might over-dribble in his desire to acquire an assist. This results in too much inactivity by the other players. This needs immediate verbal communication between coach and player and probably a video replay during the practice session. This communication between a coach and player allows the player to know what the coach thought of his performance and how it affects teamwork. This kind of communication need to occur in an open and honest manner whether the team has won or lost.

When acceptable levels of performance are obtained, individuals need praise, but suggestions for improvement must sill be afforded to the team. For example, if the big forward had ten rebounds, but only had two offensive rebounds, the coach might point out that in the next game, he needs to pay more attention to the offensive boards. Following a less than satisfactory showing, the coach needs to be much more specific. After a loss, he needs to spell out to the team where improvement is needed. He includes each person, even himself in this debriefing. Throughout this critique, positive aspects of the game still need to be pointed out and the loss must be seen and used as a leaning tool. In the face of a loss, players' confidence needs to be bolstered. The loss is viewed as only a temporary obstacle in the path of success.

Following a win or a loss, the next day should be viewed as a fresh start. The coach needs to build on success. It is a great morale booster. Remember, the team will follow the lead of the coach and is always sensitive to his moods. He is their leader. He must remain positive, confident and vigorous in the successful pursuit of his philosophy and the style of play which implements it. Everyone, whether in sports or business, has been hired as a winner.

Even during difficult times a leader needs to inspire confidence in everyone rather than sorting out the winners and losers. Remember a team is a group of individuals who win together and lose together. There are no individual winners or losers.

CHAPTER 3

GOAL SETTING

Setting up the Game Plan

And life's a race! Then dash apace
To win the olive crown!
Who wins the day may well be gay
To wear his rich renown.
Horace Spencer Fiske
"The Cycler's Song"

Adjustments to the game plan requires constant review of the team's effectiveness. Effectiveness is defined as the team's ability to meet the established goals set forth by the vision. Within the vision, three different types of goals need to be firmly established. Major goals or long term objectives provide the team with a vision towards the future. These goals serve as a long range plan and define where the team has been, where the team is right now, and where the team wants to be. They establish a framework for how the team expects to get where it wants to go. Minor goals or short term objectives narrow the focus from the broader long term objectives. These goals, which generally can be accomplished in not less than a week, and not longer than four months, assist the team in maintaining the needed intensity to accomplish the major goals. Daily goals are the third component of goal setting. These goals are very personal to each participant and serve as the most basic component to the team. In conjunction with the coach, individuals set these goals in concert with the overall plan. Daily goals may change frequently, as the needs of individuals and the team change.

In sports the setting of goals is quite easy. For a team a major goal might be winning a league championship or a tournament. Outside of sports, such goals are established in areas like productivity, excellence in performance and profit. The setting of all three types of goals serves as a road map to team success. It becomes the responsibility of all team members to establish personal goals that fit into the team's goals.

Bob Lorber and Ken Blanchard co-authored *Putting the One Minute Manager to Work* which describes a unique process to manage people. Their concept, known as the PRICE Management System, uses five principals that serve to guide managers through their supervisory interventions. Their principles of supervision may be easily adapted to our goal setting routine. P stands for pinpoint - - we need to be clear on what we want before asking or telling others. Although on the surface this appears very simplistic, often managers enter into situations without fully thinking out the situation and in some cases even regret it afterwards. The R refers to record - - or the process one needs to use to keep track of everything they need to accomplish their goal or events that can help them assess their accomplishments. With the I comes the involvement of others. As we get into the actual setting of specific goals there may be a need to involve others. These "significant others" may be people who have the resources you need to for completion of your goals or may just be able to offer an opinion that can assist you with your goals. Involvement promotes ownership of the process and buy-in to the goals. A vested interest in the goals is established in the involvement stage. C in Lorber and Blanchard's concept is the coaching that a supervisor does during a period of time prior to an evaluation. We can use the coaching as part of goal setting if we say that the job of a coach is to see the total pictures. In this regard, our goals should fit into the total organization and help the organization meet its' vision. The final letter, E, ends the goal setting with the evaluation of the goals. Periodically, we have to assess our goals and be prepared to start the process all over again. A portfolio of artifacts is collected to assess the status of the goals and where the future will take the individual and the organization.

To give you an idea on how goals are established let's look at an example from the NBA. There are eighty-two games before the playoffs begin. Before the season, a mediocre team may set getting into the playoffs as a major goal. A team which made the playoffs last year may set getting to the next round of the playoffs as a major goal. The players of contending teams say that they want "a ring" - -

symbolizing NBA supremacy. (Please note we did not use the NFL as an example. In the NFL it seems that all teams set a pre-season goal of getting to the Super Bowl. We wonder why they state this goal in this manner. Wouldn't it be better stated as "winning" the Super Bowl? Also, it is important to set an attainable goal.) These major goals are then broken down into minor goals as the NBA season is very long and the travel is extensive. A lesser goal is then established. For example, if the first ten games include four at home and six away, then set a minor goal of winning all home games and splitting the road games. During these ten games then, the minor goal would be restated as going 7 wins and 3 losses. In setting this attainable goal the team, at season's end would be a contender that would fulfill its major goal. But remember, goals must be attainable. If they are not, confusion and loss of morale can occur which create additional problems for the coach. Individual competitiveness may also decrease and loss of confidence will follow. Make the goals attainable and everyone stays focused. Daily goals help reach the minor goals. Game preparation for each of the ten encounters is well planned and gives specific attention to what each individual must do. Practice sessions give the player the drill work he needs to fulfill his role in the game plan. The team learns how to shut down the offensive strengths of the opponent and to exploit his defensive weaknesses. Such practices build confidence - - in the coach, in themselves, and the team as a unit.

Remaking an offensive play option to include a player's suggestion generates pride and confidence among team members. Asking the team members at a time out, "Who wants the shot?" in a last second game (even though the coach knows from practice sessions and previous games, who will speak out) gives players a chance to demonstrate leadership. Then, "Where do you want the ball?" precedes the coach's instructions to others regarding their roles in setting up the shooter. Team members always seem to work harder to succeed when they participate in the planning.

In following this framework of goal setting, the season or job tasks are seen as a quest that keeps team members focused. Without goals, there is a tendency to focus only on personal accomplishments rather than those contributing to the team effort. It is the coach's or leader's job to establish the goals and steer the team in that direction. Player or employee investment in the goals is not only needed, it is essential. The more personal the investment, the more likely that goals will be attained. Open communication is crucial to get this personal investment. Player or employee observations should receive careful consideration. Although the leader in our examples are always the coach or supervisor, a supervisor who only directs and never acts in a collegial and synergistic manner will never be a leader.

CHAPTER 4

FEEDBACK

Surprises infinitely great,
And little feats of high emprise,
Encouraged by a stormy cheer,
And envied by a thousand eyes.
Arthur Christopher Benson
"In the Field"

During the heat of battle, only a few minor changes can be made in your game plan. Not only does the leader not have time to break down the plan and make major adjustments, but any major changes will only confuse players. This is not time to retool or restructure, only to make small adjustments.

Staff meetings, perhaps on a daily basis, in the business world serve in a similar manner as a timeout in basketball. The first step during timeouts is to allow a short time for players to collect themselves physically to catch a quick "breath" and drink some water. This allows time to relax both physiologically and psychologically. Only after this break in the action will the players be ready to accept the feedback associated with the timeout. The coach then must be ready to give the players the necessary information for them to enhance their performances.

If the team is functioning well, timeouts serve to motivate players to continue their productive efforts. In this encouragement, the coach visualizes those things which players are doing well so that these activities are reinforced. "Bill and Luke, keep rebounding like that. That's what is getting our fast break started. Bobby, you and Lionel keep running those lanes. Dave, you're doing a good job with passing to the cutters. Keep it up!" Ten seconds of reinforcement from the coach and the players are ready to go again. If changes are needed and some small modifications are essential, players need to be told in a very direct and simple manner what each must do so that everyone quickly understands the necessary changes. Direct eye contact between coach and player is imperative when talking about the specific changes.

"They are beating us on the lob pass to O'Neill. Steve, don't front line anymore. Play him from the rear and bump him out from his post spot. We'll double team him from the passer and rotate on the pass out. Vern, your man is the passer most often, so you'll double team. Reggie, you'll have to rotate over to cover Jackson. Herb, you plug the basket. Chuck, you cover anyone at the top of the circle. Everyone set? Let's do it. No more lob passes to O'Neill." Twenty seconds is all it took to change the team's defensive tactic against the scoring post man.

At the conclusion of a time-out, a closing statement that brings everything and everybody to an effective closing has to occur. This allows the coach to check for the level of understanding the players have on the information just discussed. Once again, eye contact is the best medium to ascertain whether or not understanding has been achieved. In business, about every two weeks, another type of time out is effective. This time-out is a short wrap up that deals with general, not specific, issues just brought out by the game, or past week's performance. The coach gives a brief and honest-to-the-point message which serves as a collective evaluation.

After a win: "Great job! We kept their fast break under control by strong offensive rebounding and good transitional defense that we worked on at practice. Then we had more fast breaks than they did. You never let up. Nice work."

The coach picks out several positive factors even if a loss has occurred. In that case, mention the main cause for the loss. "That's a tough loss. We moved the ball well enough and got the shots we wanted - - that was on the plus side. We didn't stop their post-up game, though. We've got to do better with that. We'll work on it more at practice so that our double teams are quicker. We'll be ready for them next time." In each case, the time-outs should have an established time limit which assists the coach and participants to remain focused. During the game, the time out is 20 seconds or a full time-out established by rule. Post game wrap-ups should take no longer than a few minutes.

The post game locker room also provides an opportunity for the coach to visit each player individually to give a short appraisal of his work in the game. It is also necessary to spend time with those who may not have played in the game. A word of explanation, if it seems necessary, or a short encouragement for these players shows them that they are not being forgotten. There will probably be a time when these players are needed and the coach must keep them mentally and physically ready. There are going to be times other than those previously mentioned when the coach will need to call time outs. In basketball, it may be at a practice session on non-game days. Whether the team is winning or losing, these time-outs will reinforce the game plan and vision. Specific feedback should be given to each player in a personal atmosphere. Make sure that no one is left out, especially those who did not play the night before. At some point during these time-outs, players need to be given the opportunity to air opinions as to what's going right, what's going wrong and how things can be better. When valid criticism is offered from an individual source, the coach needs to share that information with the other team members at the next group meeting. These personal, one-on-one chats serve as an excellent time to talk about skill development. This assists everyone in understanding their role on the team and fosters the concept that everyone contributes to the success of the team.

Practicing your skills and role playing are good activities during these time-outs. Even in the NBA, where the best players in the world play their sport, not a day should pass without some practice on improving basic skills. During these times, the coach offers quality information and instruction to the player that the player finds will improve his performance. Successful team players practice their skills constantly. As a player Larry Bird, of the Boston Celtics, even practiced his high level shooting skills on a daily basis. Even before the lights were fully on at the arena, and a couple of hours before game time, Bird would take a hundred or more of the shots he felt he would get in the coming game. Perfection of performance is never left to chance.

More intense feedback is provided at the full length practice session. Before the practice begins, the group is called together. The purpose of the practice is outlined. The game is broken down into its most basic parts and special emphasis is given to areas of weakness that have been uncovered during recent games. During the practice, periodic breaks need to occur to debrief the players on the progress of the practice session. At the debriefing, great attention needs to be paid to the things that are not going as well as expected in the practice. This needs to be in a straight forward manner. "Let's stop it here. This drill is to give everyone practice in defending the driver and forcing him to the baseline. Three of the last four drivers have gotten to the lane. Pick up your concentration. Let's get this job done right."

Knowing as much as possible about the players can assist the coach during these interventions. In fact, motivational inventory tests like the AMI referred to in an earlier chapter, or similar instruments can help managers in this area. Dr. Ogilvie's work with the TrailBlazers helped us. As a result of such test information that is shared simultaneously with player and coach, a common bond is shared by the two. The coach learns which players he can drive hard and which he can prod; which players need constant reinforcement of confidence and which have an ample supply; which players want to lead and which would rather follow. Armed with this information, the coach and more appropriately influence each of the players on the team. Some players may be suspicious or skeptical of how the information will be used. However, if trust has been established, the coach is "up-front" with the uses of the test, and the results are privately discussed, then it will be seen by the participants as a way to improve their performance. Whatever negativism there may be, quickly disappear.

Dr. Morris Massey, formerly of the University of Colorado and an international presenter, gives us additional assistance in understanding human behavior. Massey's theory is that it is up to the leader to find out as much information about the individual's past. These areas include one's family structure, friends, where he grew up, financial status, type of schooling, religious affiliation and other influential items that he was exposed to as a child. Using this information, the leader can structure different approach strategies in dealing with these individuals based on their learned value structure. Many leaders have used this technique very successfully to plan for meetings, running time-outs, performance reviews and dealing with company policy.

The coach or supervisor does not strive to play the role of friend or father to the team member during time-outs. In fact, team members have to recognize the coach's role as "the coach" or the supervisor. Any relationships that develop are developed because of the ability of the coach and players to perform their jobs. What develops from being yourself is a kind of transparency. The respect you receive from your team is because the team accepts you for what you are. Any relationships that develop will do so naturally. As we have stated previously, it is extremely important to remember that a mutually respectful relationship is critical for the team's success and if the players like you and you like them consider it a bonus.

John Madden and Chuck Fairbanks are two very successful former coaches who, while being themselves, show opposing techniques of communications. It was interesting to observe Madden, while coaching the NFL Raiders, managed his large group of players by being well organized and his outgoing style of communication. Throughout his coaching, Madden seemed to visualize what he would see when he walked onto the practice field. He set up his organization in such a manner that practice was conducted in small groups. During the practice, he would spend time with each group and as practice closed, he spoke to the entire team collectively. You would sense a high level of organization with a corresponding level of meaningful activity.

Chuck Fairbanks, while coaching the NFL Patriots, organized another highly defined structure. Fairbanks surrounds himself with a cadre of confidants who were good communicators. The difference in style is that, unlike Coach Madden, Fairbanks seldom talked to his players. All communication went through the assistant coaches. He saw no need to communicate directly with the players but yet was very successful.

Certainly these are examples of differing techniques, but both individuals were very successful. A coach must develop his communication technique in a style which he feels ease and comfort. It must be his style and not that of someone else. Often when looking at styles, it's sometimes hard to believe what can really work. The key elements of effective communication are good organization, and honesty and clarity of presentation. These time- tested principles allow feedback to be given in an open and honest fashion without destroying relationships when the feed back may be negative. Dr. Stephen Covey uses the analogy of a bank account, where you will never be overdrawn if you make sufficient deposits.

Dr. Covey states that we all have an emotional bank account too. If we all make sufficient "deposits" to one another, such as praise, thank you's and helping one another, to mention a few, than when correction is needed and a "withdrawal" occurs the relationship won't be lost. The good results that follow should surprise no one. Every successful person wants timely and constructive feedback. Every champion always wants to improve. It is the job of the leader to develop an individual feedback system for everyone they come in contact which promotes professional and personal growth within the team.

CHAPTER 5

THE TEAM

The Final Result

We crown thee, Hero, not for strength alone; ...
Strength in the base is objectless, inert,
Or strained to keep some passion on its throne.
Edward Cracrost Lefroy
"At the Isthmian Games"

Webster's definition of teamwork is "work done by several associates with each doing a part, but all subordinating personal prominence to the efficiency of the whole." In an effective team no one subordinates himself, since each person is working as hard as possible to maximize the efficiency of the group. There is everyone working in a collegial atmosphere. In a true team we are not asking individuals to subordinate their talents, but rather to maximize their efforts. It is up to the coach to establish how the abilities of his players are to be best utilized through the establishment of roles to be played.

When this process occurs, there is a sense that the team is on track to reach its goal. This happened with the Portland TrailBlazers during my (Ramsay's) first season there. The TrailBlazers had never had a .500 record had never made the playoffs before. During training camp of that season, it was evident from the players' actions that the TrailBlazers were on the edge of being a great team. You could just feel the cohesiveness, the team work and the high level of play. On an especially sharp practice day, the coach stopped the action and gathered the team around him. "We are playing great basketball today. If we can maintain this level of play, there is no limit on what we can do this year," he told them. The team needed to hear this from their coach because while this kind of success was not familiar to them, he had coached NBA playoff teams before. The coach used that occasion to build team confidence.

How did this happen? W.as it by accident? Certainly not! As stated previously, many components enter into the picture of success. Having the right mix of personnel is essential. The Trail Blazers had this kind of mix. Maurice Lucas and Bob Gross were a perfect combination of power and speed at the forward positions. Guards Dave Twardzik and Lionel Hollins complimented each other's defensive play making and scoring skills and the great Bill Walton was the hub of the action. There was also a bench deep with role players who supplied their skills whenever needed. Something more nebulous was also present. There was a sense of togetherness, a sensitivity among players, and the enjoyment of just playing well together as a team. (It is also amazing to note that nearly 30 years later only basketball aficionados recognize all but one of the names – an excellent team does not have to make up by All-Stars but everyone helping one another to achieve.)

All of us in management have studied Maslow's *Hierarchy of Needs*. This entire team was at the top of the pyramid, self-actualization. Once this was verified by the coach, it became his task to keep is high level of confidence. As success is experienced, it's imperative to maintain a feeling of being unbeatable. This team became the only NBA team ever to win the championship after having failed to make a previous playoff position. In the 1976-77 season, the TrailBlazers defeated the favored Philadelphia Seventy-Sixers in the championship series, 4-2. The TrailBlazers became World Champions! The following season, although not repeating as champions, the TrailBlazers succeeded at attaining a 50-10 record after 60 regular-season games before a rash of injuries beset the team. What set this apart from other teams was its high level of team play and the effective joint action of all involved - - the starting team, reserve players, the coaches and the team trainer.

This team, hopefully aided by its coach, had a visible goal, a clear game plan and know what role each individual had to play for the team to be successful. If these factors are all in harmony, and there is a coordination of effort, not only can team performance reach a level of excellence, but performance under pressure will be enhanced. This, in turn, enables the team to win the tough, close games - - the games that go down to the wire and are decided in the final few seconds. If this is not happening, there may be a need for minor modification of the game plan. Simple modification is better than complex changes. Shortening the procedure gives better results than expanding it.

Sometimes unhealthy competition between team members surfaces. This problem must be addressed quickly. If that is the case, the coach must re clarify roles with the vying player so that they work again toward team goals. The sooner that situation is resolved, the better it is for team unity and rapport. Unhealthy competition is often due to a lack of communication.

A healthy team is always talking...at practice, during the game on and off the court. On the championship team at Portland, you couldn't keep Bill Walton quiet - - nor would you want to. He was a master at good healthy communication on the court. From his defensive position near the basket, he was constantly directing defensive adjustments, "Watch the backpick, Bobby", "I've got the basket, Luke", "Get through, Dave". Bill was very succinct - - nothing unnecessary, just the right words at the right time. Good communication fosters mutual understanding and respect among team members. The TrailBlazers were great communicators. Team members may even have different life styles outside of work, but if there is effective communication on the job, they are viewed as a singular working unit.

The coach is an important component of the internal communications network. It is a sensitive position. As the leader of the team, he must choose to avoid interaction with any team member if it jeopardizes team success. For example, the coach won't listen to any personal criticism of another team member unless both players are present. When the two parties are present the coach resolves the differences between them. These types of discussions can be beneficial. They clear the air and help to restore team unity. All players can't be expected to feel alike at all times. If the team is the beneficiary of this kind of intervention by the coach, then it is another example of positive communication.

A healthy team is a team that is dedicated and directed to meeting the team goals. An unhealthy team tends to focus on individual skills and tends to have team members compete for individual rewards which are outside the team goals. For example, a player may state that he's going to win the league scoring title. However, statistics show that the team with the scoring leader seldom wins. In such an instance, the coach may want to intervene and redirect the player's personal goal to fit better what will benefit the team the most. A player with the potential to lead the league in scoring certainly has much to give to the team's offense. The coach must get this asset from the player and yet keep him focused on team goals.

A good illustration of this is Michael Jordan, generally acknowledged to be the most highly skilled basketball player to have played the game and, arguably, the best ever. For all the accolades that have come his way, Jordan had to change his game in order to play for an NBA champion. He had to be less intent on scoring high numbers than he was on winning a championship. Once the skill level of his teammates improved, the championships were a natural result. Regardless of his great, great talent - - he cannot do it all by himself. But his goal was to win the championship - - not the individual awards. But in winning the championships personal accolades also followed including the league leading scorer and first team all defense in the same season.

When we appeal to a player's pride, the right approach must be taken. Each player has a different level of acceptance of what we have to say to him. Ken Blanchard, author and international consultant with Paul Hersey developed a highly effective model for use in approaching people about change. They focus on four styles with which to confront people. They call the technique "Situational Leadership II". Blanchard and Hersey state that people have varying degrees of acceptance of what you tell them based on their own personality. They say that in certain cases, the leader needs to provide specific instructions and examples. The leader also needs to closely supervise the individual's task accomplishment.

A second individual may need a leader to direct and supervise task accomplishment but may also need a leader who will explain decisions, solicit suggestions and supports progress. Style three requires a leader who will facilitate, praise and encourage a subordinate's efforts toward task accomplishment but also begin to allow the subordinate to take some responsibility for decision-making. Finally, there are some to whom the leader can turn over all decision-making and problem solving. If we change "leader" to "coach" and "subordinates" to "players", we can really see how this concept can apply to our efforts to establish a strong team either in athletics or the world of business.

The coach can appeal to the player's sense of pride to help create this atmosphere of acceptance. The effective team has a high degree of productivity. It wins consistently, there is visible team unity. There is a great rapport between players and coaches. There is a willingness to sacrifice individual personal goals to make the team stronger. There is a high degree of loyalty and dependability. All of these qualities promote the bottom line - - reaching for and achieving the major goals established by the coach or leader. A good visual which can assist in remembering the team concept is your hand. If you hold your hand open all your fingers are going in different directions. This would represent a dysfunctional team or one that only cares about individual efforts. As you close your hand into a fist a powerful vehicle is established, one based on unity. This unity produces a level of organizational effectiveness that can only be accomplished through individuals working collectively, a team.

CHAPTER 6

WHAT'S NEXT?

What to Do in the Off Season

Sleep, sleep,
By your mountains steep,
Or down where the prairie grasses sweep!
For soft is the song my paddle sings
E. Pauline Johnson
"The Song My Paddle Sings"

William Glasser, a California psychiatrist, believes that human behavior can be managed through a concept known as "Control Theory". At the center of his concept is the leader's job of making sure that the basic needs of the team members have been fulfilled and if they are not to develop a scheme to be sure that they are fulfilled. Only after these needs are satisfied - - each of them having equal importance - - is the person able to be a productive member of the group. Glasser's basic needs are survival, power, belonging, freedom, love and fun. The previous chapters' contents can all be directed to your fulfilling these basic needs for members of your team. The fact that everyone has a chance based on his skills, to determine his role, helps team members feel that they can survive. Players who feel free to discuss team matters and participate in goal setting exercises fulfill the need for power. Team unity and effective time-outs establish a sense of belonging. Allowing individuals to play a specific role within the framework of the team, gives them a sense of freedom. Feedback, if the appropriate approach is used, an open, honest communication satisfy the need for love, while being part of a winning team makes it all fun. The measure of success is directly correlated to the satisfaction of the basic needs of your team and to your ability in implementing the qualities of a good leader.

Although your own self evaluation is related to the success of the team, your future success is related to the success of the team and several other important factors. First, is your mind open to new ideas? Often successful people view change as inappropriate and to entertain a new idea is seen as here say. Times change, people change and new ideas should be analyzed as a way to become better at what you do. Second, as you become and maintain a certain level of winning, do you develop a sense of complacency? Complacency can lead to a lower level of achievement and a reduction in quality just around the corner. To remain successful, but not the best, has to always remain distasteful. Third, are you willing to be a servant to those you lead? Recently, the concept of "servant leadership" adds a new dimension to how we lead. It relies on the leader to constantly strive to serve the needs of those they are leading. This is not to say to forget about accountability but to always remember that you are dealing with another important human being. Principles such as always maintaining your own sense of ethics; trust, patience, sense of value and honesty and others that have withstood the test of time assist you in this servant role. A great example can be found in Halberstam's book *Firehouse* in which the officers in the Fire Department of New York (FDNY) subscribe to a code of honor and pride. The unwritten code that the officers follow is that they are always first in and last out at a fire, always acting as servants to the fireman and firewomen they lead. Fourth, do you become irrational in the face of defeat? If you do, you may not be keeping things in perspective. Balance in your own life is necessary to remain a winner.

Even good coaches may lose this balance because, like thoroughbred race horses, they are on edge. Because coaches are on edge, they view each call by the officials as game-deciding. Through the eyes of the coach, referees make many bad calls and always, it seems, against his team. (As the role of the coach changes to that of television or radio analyst, the calls really aren't all that bad.)

Once, during a TrailBlazer game, the coach thought that the referees were making many calls that were going against his team. The coach reacted by focusing his emotions on the officials. Then, at a time-out, the coach delivered another verbal salvo toward the officials before turning to his players. As the coach approached them,

Bill Walton had presence to say, "Coach, don't you know that we don't play well when you do that?" This statement brought the coach quickly to the reality of his role. He realized with sudden clarity, that if he wanted a poised team, the coach had better demonstrate that quality himself.

It is important to recognize that there are certain fights that you will win, and some that you'll lose, no matter how hard you try. Selecting your goals carefully and knowing how to accept defeat are important aspects of keeping things in balance. Dr. Hans Selye, once a medical doctor at the University of Montreal, and considered by many to be the father of stress management, states this very well. "Fight for highest attainable goals, but don't put up resistance in vain." In this statement, Selye alludes to his "fight or flight" response that causes stress to be seen by people as either a positive or negative force in their life. Most often, we have to fight the battle, but sometimes it's possible to just fly away and escape the conflict. For some it is better to escape a devastating loss by not fighting the battle. For coaches and many other leaders, there is not such escape hatch. They must forget the losing battle, accept the defeat, learn from it, and gird themselves for the next fray. A good method of preparing for the next encounter is to find some kind of healthy diversion that enables the leader to continue on in a positive direction.

To get away from the demands and concentrations of the job, a daily physical workout, started only after a complete physical by your doctor, will help to dissipate tensions. Exercise, not only affords positive physiological results, like reduced cholesterol, blood pressure levels and risk of heart disease, but it also promotes positive psychological factors. It affords you the opportunity to regain your composure and reset your sights so that a positive attitude prevails. Activities such as swimming, running on a track or treadmill, biking, rowing, or brisk walking are excellent rejuvenators. Doing this for at least a half an hour each day helps to maintain an emotional equilibrium, and to eat and rest better. Personal relationships improve because there is a better feeling of self.

In the area of physical well-being it is important to eat properly. Simply stated, one wants to avoid fried and fatty foods, and to concentrate on lean meats and fish, plenty of vegetables, fruits and grains. By drinking six to eight glasses of water each day, one is assured of a balanced, healthy diet which in turn generates productive performance. Avoiding drugs and excesses in alcohol are also vital to good health and well-being.

Picking up a good book to read on a subject that interests you is also a great leisure activity. Whether the book is history or fiction, fact or fantasy, this activity can serve as a great respite from the day's activities. Music, theater, movies or other activities in the arts can also be beneficial. It is also important to spend quality time with your family or loved one. These activities can be done without guilt feelings and the result is a balanced life. This is complete living, but it is not easily attained by a leader's hard driven life to succeed.

To those leaders, success is so important that it becomes an all-consuming passion, leaving little time in their lives for anything or anyone else. These are difficult people to counsel, but inevitably they reach a point in life when they "take time to smell the roses".

Complete living is a very satisfying result of your endeavors. The basis of this satisfaction is in the professional and personal success attained combined with a sense of expanding horizons. Maintaining your focus on goal setting and skill development, while maintaining your perspective of life is the key to success. Rosenthal and Jacobson in *Pygmaleon in the Classroom*, talk of the self-fulfilling prophecy: if you think positive thoughts, positive things will happen; while, if you think negative thoughts, those things will certainly happen.

Go forward today thinking good thoughts. Be reminded of the classic example of the power of positive thinking set forth in the children's book *The Little Engine That Could* - - "I think I can, I think I can, I know I can".

After researching and writing this book we found that many of our words and statements are original yet many of them are connected to fabulous teachers, organizational development specialists and leaders in the field of leadership and motivation. What we have found to be most interesting is the interdependency of all these thoughts. All the examples and models have relationships that transcend the boundaries of time and place where they were first developed and applied. The authors of these works, including those of this book, each have a technique that urges the reader to adapt and apply these models to their life.

The two pictures that follow help describe the relationships and dependency between all that we and the other authors describe as ways to "coach" and motivate people. We choose to call this graphic organizer the Core of Leadership. You will see that the roots provide a foundation for the fruit of our labors. These roots are comprised of our personal and organizational values, the alignment of these values, our own sense of strength and our own desire to seek personal and professional excellence. If our values are not aligned and we do not have a true sense of commitment the tree will not be nourished to provide the fruit. Our own life-tested principles ground the tree that holds the fruit while the core of the fruit is made up of motivation, accountability and leadership style. This core allows not only for the seeds of the future to develop but also when they are used to influence our personal style will allow our subordinate relationships to be nurtured and grow as we become more effective as leaders. This is truly a blend of ideas including our own while at the same time it uses the time tested principles of Dr. Stephen Covey, Dr. Ken Blanchard and Dr. Bob Lorber, Dr. Tom Peters, Dr. Morris Massey and Phil Jackson among many others. We urge all the readers of our book to seek out the works listed in the bibliography to gain insight to each of these heroes of leadership and develop a style which works for you and your position.

Information regarding motivational presentations on these concepts can be obtained by sending an e-mail to butrfly2003@comcast.net.

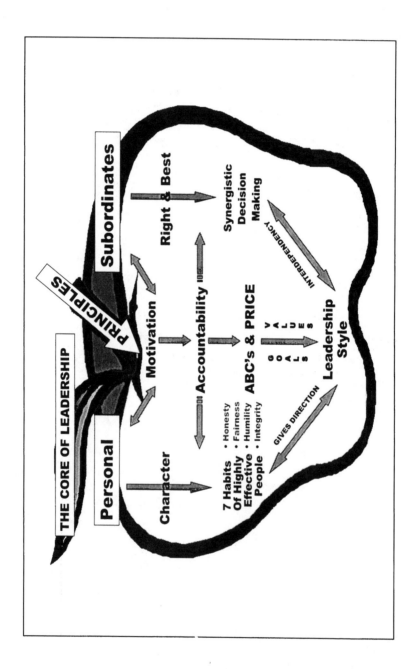

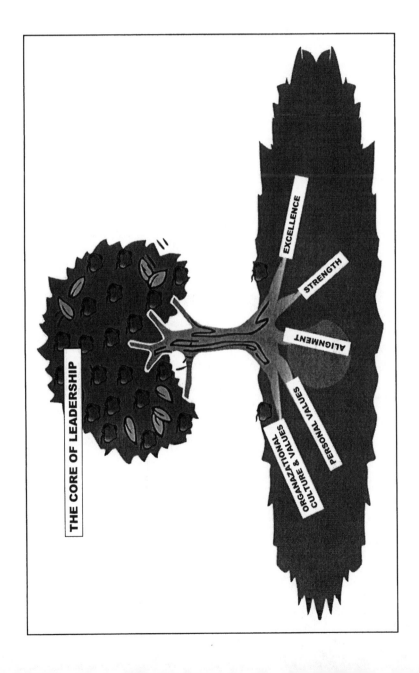

AFTERWORD

The project of writing *Coaching for Performance Improvement* began over ten years ago. Over this ten-year period priorities for both of us were in a state of flux. Many times we worked on the manuscript and many more times we put the manuscript away. About a year ago we picked it up one more time and decided to complete the book. Our initial thoughts were that nothing had to change but when reviewing the manuscript we realized that some things have changed that needed revision. This was particularly true with some of the examples we used that had to be changed from the present tense to the past tense. So we made these changes but also found that a major thing never changed over the years and probably will never change regardless of the passing years to come. As we reviewed the contents what we noticed through our examples was that the major theme throughout the book is service to the stakeholders. We will use the word stakeholder to describe anyone we come in contact with, our family and friends, our peers, our subordinates and supervisor, and our customers (anyone who relies on us for something- we guess that's really everybody).

The major theme that we noticed in both the examples that we used and the literature we used to support the examples is the theme of being of service to others. This becomes very interesting as it almost creates a spiritual dimension to leadership, for example in the Jesuit tradition "A man for others". In addition it seems that in all positive examples of leadership the leader seems to have developed a relationship of mutual respect. This reciprocal respect seems to be obtained through the leader's ability to be of service or a servant to those they supervise. We mention this concept only briefly in Chapter 6 but thought that after our critical review of our book that it is important to give some additional time to this important theme especially when today it seems in direct conflict with a "what's in it for me" mentality.

The theme of serving others goes well beyond the scope of coaching and leadership and goes far into changing the world in which we live should we choose to practice the principals. Robert Greenleaf, the founder in 1969 of The Greenleaf Center for Servant-Leadership, first began to speak and write about what seemed to be a non-traditional approach to leadership. This approach was the belief that an individual and/or organizations goals and margins could be obtained or exceeded when the leader sincerely promoted a collegial work environment. Once again, this isn't a novel idea but notice that it becomes novel as most leaders and their organizations do not practice this approach. There always appears on the surface the expression of this approach, often in the mission statement or vision, but very often the approach is not practiced. In fact there is a major United States government agency that has a statement placed prominently in every office stating, "People are our most Valuable Resource". We are sure you can already guess what we are going to say next- from our experience and in fact from data taken from employee attitude surveys of that agency they do not practice what they preach.

The spirit of serving can be found in many life examples of many leaders. Many coaches, executives and parents are tough but still love the people they are directly involved with supervising. Some coaches are very demanding yet show respect and love to their players. One of our friends Coach Jim Baron (currently coaching the University of Rhode Island Rams), is a Servant-Leader in all respects of the concept, he truly loves his players. Jim is extremely demanding on his student athletes as evidenced through the hard practices and grueling film reviews and schedule they are forced to keep. On the other hand he is a loving human being who truly shields his student athletes from harm. He is sure to provide them study time to aid in their academic success, reaches out to them in their times of personal need, shares holidays with them when they can't get home, helps them set attainable goals and invites them to be part of his family. He treats his players, coaches, family and friends this way- he is always there for them even at the expense of his time and sometimes his own personal space. In return he gets the same from his players, family and friends; loyalty, hard work and dedication to what is best for the program or relationship. One wonders if this could ever be achieved without the servant first serving others.

Every sport has examples of a taskmaster who is respected and loved because of the respect and love they first give to others.

Several friends in the world of baseball also have these qualities, Jeff Manto (currently a minor league hitting coordinator for the Pittsburgh Pirates) and Tom Filer (currently a pitching coach for the Philadelphia Phillies organization). These gentleman balance hard work with positive relationships and love for their players to get players to be successful. Baseball is an unusual sport where being successful 25% of the time for a hitter can lead to promotions. All the failure can also lead to second guessing yourself as a player and the need for the coach to be a nurturer of champions. Egos can be very fragile and if the ego is broken a career can be ended. These two leaders once again exhibit qualities that allow them to place rigorous demands on their players yet command respect and hard work from the individuals they supervise. The common qualities that both have is the love for what they do and the love they give to their players. If anyone is uncomfortable with the use of the word love another four-letter word, care, can be substituted. But in any case this common quality is the respect that the leader has for every aspect of the players life without being perceived by the player as just the coach butting into their lives. How do Jeff and Tom do this, we think is safe to say, that they have a balance in their own lives that allow them to serve as role models by placing demands on themselves before placing any respectful demands on others. This also transcends the boundary of work into their personal life.

We believe that all three examples serve as models for all leaders- the ability to make high-level demands of others and those to whom the demands are being made having a deeply imbedded trust in the leader so that they will follow the leaders directions. This can be transferred into the world of everyday employment or your personal life. The parent, teacher, police officer, office manager, supervisor, doctor, judge and the list goes on of today cannot expect blind obedience from anyone they come in contact with. It seems like the question of the day is "why" and the answer cannot be "because I said so" or "because that's the way it's always been". Each directive has to be sold to the individual or group unless of course the decision is a life or death decision that has a sense of immediacy attached to it. The selling is not the typical sale but rather a part ownership in the decision making process, synergistic decision-making. It involves the leader reducing the power obtained from their position and sharing the power with their players or employees. If the servant relationship exists it isn't giving up power but rather sharing the decision-making. The most powerful outcome is still the decision that you want will exist because you are not only seen as the expert to your people but the relationship fosters your people making or suggesting the same decision that you would have made. This outcome can only be achieved through the powerful relationship gained through serving others. By the way, we would be remiss if we didn't mention that even when immediate decisions need to be made it is extremely important as a servant leader to debrief after the event is over as to why the decision was made the way it was and ask for input on how the situation should be handled in the future.

Wouldn't it be magnificent if when your players are on the court or field or your employees at work when you are not around are making decisions that you could be proud of? It is our belief that the servant style will promote these occurrences and "Loyalty to the Absent" will become a normal part of your life. This loyalty can only happen if you set your course in the right direction or as Dr. Covey so clearly states in the *Seven Habits of Highly Effective People* when he talks of taking care of your private victories. You have to be secure in yourself to be the servant. You have to be willing to give of yourself even to people who you don't like or don't like you. You have to be tireless in the mentoring role that you have to play even to those who you believe should know better. You have to have a passion for life and work or as Horst Schulze (retired CEO of the Ritz Carlton Hotels) so beautifully stated " The reason I go to work everyday is to be with my friends and to make the organization better". You have to be willing to try and fail while you give others the courage to try and fail. You have to be prepared to find ways to build confidence in people who may be insecure or have just made a mistake. You have to be willing to hold people accountable even if you like them or are friends with them, tough love. You have to be willing to take a stand for what is right and not be swayed by the moment or the immediate return. Ethics always are instilled your decision and those who you lead. You have to be willing to make decisions that may not be popular but you realize are what is best for your people. You have to celebrate successes and know your people- be a cheerleader for them. You have to give them credit for these successes and should they fail protect them from those who could hurt them (in athletics this is often the media and in life it could be from themselves or your supervisor). And we are sure that we have left out a few "You....".

We would like now to go back to the beginning of our book, "so you want to be a leader" and add instead "before you can consider being a leader you must first learn to serve". After one is ready to serve than and only than does the rest of the book make sense. In serving others the others will walk confidently and proudly and while naturally making themselves successful will also make you successful. With this responsibility to serve and the benefits, which you, personally, gain by it, comes an awesome responsibility to give back. It is our belief that it is our obligation to give back to the stakeholders what you have learned or received monetarily. If you are always receiving (taking) and not giving back to society your concept of servant leadership is being somewhat skewed, isn't it? If this giving back were to occur the concept of leadership could ultimately change society and the world. Conceivably personal and corporate greed would be reduced for the benefit of the world. Who knows maybe the Beetles were right all along, "All you need is Love".

TAO OF LEADERSHIP

Leaders are best
     When people scarcely know they exist
Not so good when people obey and acclaim them
Worst when people despise them
Fail to honor people they fail to honor you
But of good leaders who talk little
When their work is done, task fulfilled
People will say: we have done this Ourselves!
            Verse 17
            Tao Te Ching

BIBLIOGRAPHY
AND
SUGGESTED READINGS

Autry, James, *Love and Profit*, New York, Avon Books, 1991.

Blanchard, Kenneth H., et.al., *Situational Leadership II*, Escondido, CA, Blanchard Training and Development, Inc., 1985.

Blanchard, Kenneth and Johnson, Spenser, *The One Minute Manager*, New York, William Morrow and Company, 1981.

Blanchard, Kennth and Lorber, Robert, *Putting the One Minute Manager to Work*, New York, William Morrow and Company, 1981.

Bradley, Bill, *Values of the Game*, New York, Artisan, 1998.

Clark, D.B., *Alexander Pope*, New York, Twayne Publishers, 1967.

Collins, Jim, *Good to Great*, New York, Harper Business, 2001.

Covey, Sean, *The Seven Habits of Highly Effective Teens*, New York, Fireside, 1998.

Covey, Stephen R., *First Things First*, New York, Simon and Schuster, 1994.

Covey, Stephen R., *Principle – Centered Leadership*, New York, Simon and Schuster, 1991.

Covey, Stephen R., Merrill, A. Roger, Jones, Dewitt, *The Nature of Leadership*, Salt Lake City, Franklin Covey, 1998.

Covey, Stephen R., *The Seven Habits of Highly Effective People*, New York, Simon and Schuster, 1990.

Franklin, Kenneth H., *The Executive's Guide to Health and Fitness*, Fairfield, NJ, The Economics Press, 1985.

Fulghum, Robert, *Words I Wish I Wrote*, New York, Cliff Street Books, 1997.

Glasser, William, *Control Theory*, New York, Harper and Row, 1984.

Halberstam, David, *Firehouse*, New York Hyperion, 2002.

Huizinga, Johan, *Homo Ludens: A Study of the Play Element in Culture*, Boston, The Beacon Press, 1955.

Hunter, James C., *The Servant*, Roseville, CA, Prima, 1998.

Jackson, Phil, *Sacred Hoops*, New York, Hyperion, 1995.

Jacobson, Edmond, *You Must Relax*, New York, McGraw-Hill, 1978.

Jandt, Fred, *Win-Win Negotiations*, New York, John Wiley and Sons, 1985.

Massey, Morris, *The People Puzzle*, Reston, VA Reston Publishing Co., Inc., 1979.

Moore, Robert, *Sports and Mental Health*, Springfield, IL, Charles C. Thomas, 1966.

Oncken, Jr. William, *Managing Management Time*, Englewood Cliffs, NJ, Prentice Hall, 1984.

Peters, Tom, *Reinventing Work*, New York, Knopf, 1999.

Peters, Tom, *The Pursuit of WOW*, New York, Vantage Books, 1994.

Peters, Tom, *Thriving on Chaos*, New York, Alfred A. Knopf, 1987.

Piper, Watty, *Little Engine That Could*, New York Putnam Group, 1984.

Rice, Wallace, *The Athlete's Garland*, Chicago, A.C. McClurg and Co., 1905.

Roberson, J.R., *Japan: from Shogun to SONY*, New York, Atheneum, 1985.

Scott, Jack, *The Athletic Revolution*, New York, The Free Press, 1971.

Selye, Hans, *The Stress of Life*, New York, McGraw-Hill, 1966.

Smith, Hyrum, *What Matters Most*, New York, Simon and Schuster, 2000.

Smith, Hyrum, *The Modern Gladiator*, Salk Lake City, UT, Franklin Covey Publishing, 2001.

Spears, Larry C., et.al., editors, *Focus on Leadership*, New York, John Wiley, 2002.

The Performance Book, Plymouth, MI, Human Synergistics, 2003.

Webster's New Collegiate Dictionary, Springfield, MA, G. and C. Merriam Co., 1973.

ABOUT

THE AUTHORS

Dr. Jack Ramsay is currently the ESPN radio color analyst for NBA games of the week and an International Ambassador for Basketball for the NBA. He is a graduate of St. Joseph's University and holds a doctor's degree in Educational Administration from the University of Pennsylvania. He has served as a high school basketball coach for 6 years, a college basketball coach for 11 years and an NBA coach for 20 years winning a world championship with the Portland TrailBlazers. He is the author of several books including *Dr. Jack's Leadership Lessons Learned from Basketball*, a fitness buff and delivers motivational presentations at all levels. He resides in Ocean City, New Jersey.

Dr. Jim Lynch is currently a school administrator and Adjunct Assistant Professor at Widener University School of Education and Adjunct Lecturer at Holy Family University School of Education and Business Administration. He is a graduate of Kean College of New Jersey and holds a doctor's degree in Educational Theory from Rutgers, The State University of New Jersey. He has served as the Director of Cherokee Consultants, an organizational and human resource group that designs and delivers training and motivational programs across the country. He is the co-author of *Excellence Now...and for the Future* along with several journal articles. He resides in Medford, New Jersey.